Thinking About College

YOUR FIRST
YEAR OF COLLEGE
FROM CLASSROOM TO DORM ROOM

Maria DaSilva-Gordon

ROSEN
PUBLISHING®

New York

Dedicated to my father who made my journey through college possible. I could not have done it without you. To my family and friends, thank you for your love and support

Published in 2010 by The Rosen Publishing Group, Inc.
29 East 21st Street, New York, NY 10010

First Edition

Library of Congress Cataloging-in-Publication Data

DaSilva-Gordon, Maria.
Your first year of college: from classroom to dorm room / Maria DaSilva-Gordon.
   p. cm. — (Thinking about college) (First edition)
Includes bibliographical references and index.
ISBN 978-1-4358-3600-6 (library binding)
ISBN 978-1-4358-8506-6 (pbk)
ISBN 978-1-4358-8507-3 (6 pack)
1. College student orientation — United States. I. Title.
LB2343.32.D37 2010
378.1'98 — dc22

2009015473

Manufactured in Malaysia

CPSIA Compliance Information: Batch #TWW10YA: For Further Information contact Rosen Publishing, New York, New York at 1-800-237-9932

Contents

Introduction

What does college life look like?

If you think it resembles high school, think again. One of the major differences between college and high school is the level of the academics. Whether you plan to attend a technical school, community college, or four-year institution, your college experience will include classes that are more challenging. The workload of these courses will be more demanding than high school homework. Fortunately, even if you didn't graduate at the top of your high school class, you can still succeed in college by getting organized, staying focused, and using the skills discussed in this book.

Compared to high school, the college experience typically offers more diversity in terms of the student population. With people from various backgrounds attending college, you'll be exposed to ideas, perspectives, and traditions that are different from your own. Interacting with a diverse group of people is a major part of the college learning experience—and a rewarding one. Getting involved in activities outside of the classroom is one of the ways you can meet new people. You'll have lots of options when it comes to extracurricular activities, from clubs to internships to community service.

As a college student, you'll also be making many more decisions on your own, from choosing what classes to take to deciding

College courses are not only more challenging than high school classes, they also tend to be larger. Above, students attend a college lecture.

what foods to eat. But with more freedom and decision-making opportunities comes accountability. You'll be responsible for the results of your decisions, and any consequences will be yours. There's a good chance you'll make mistakes along the way. The important thing is to learn from them. And remember, you are not alone when facing the challenges of college life. There are many resources available both on and off campus.

Navigating your first year of college can be tricky at times. The information within this book can help to guide you. Be curious. Be open-minded. Be responsible. Although college is more demanding than high school, its rewards are that much greater.

Chapter 1

Acing Academics

How is college different from high school when it comes to academics? The courses are not only more challenging, they also move at a faster pace. College classes tend to be larger, and professors may not be able to assess whether or not everyone in a big lecture hall understands the lesson. You'll be expected to do more reading, writing, and homework. Attendance usually isn't enforced, and the professor isn't going to remind you about upcoming papers or tests.

What does all of this mean for you? College requires responsibility. It's up to you to attend class, review lessons, manage deadlines, and complete the coursework. You're in charge. Unlike in high school, you won't get daily reminders to do your homework or go to class. It's also up to you to ask for help if you need it. Fortunately, there are plenty of resources. You can reach out to your professors or an academic advisor. You can seek advice from upperclassmen or your peers. You can also turn to your college's academic support center for help.

Time Management Tips

In his book *Making the Most of College*, Professor Richard Light shared findings from a decade of in-depth interviews with more than 1,600 Harvard undergraduates. His study found that students

Getting a Head Start

Going from high school studies to college academics can be a shocking experience. Fortunately, there are things you can do now to make the transition smoother.

Reading. You'll be doing a lot more reading in college. Get yourself used to a larger reading load by reading daily, anything from newspapers to novels. You'll keep your brain active by exploring topics that interest you, and you'll build a stronger vocabulary for college.

Taking Notes. In college, you'll be expected to take notes during lectures and discussions and while reading. Practice by jotting down notes that capture the essence of what you read. Test different note-taking techniques until you find the best one for you. For examples, see the Web links related to this book.

Writing. Term papers and essays are just some of the types of writing you'll be expected to do in college. Sharpen your writing skills by maintaining a journal, writing letters to friends, or regularly blogging about a topic. Try crafting a creative short story, a humorous essay, or an opinion piece about a current movie or news event. Also, improve your writing by adding to your vocabulary. Each week, select an unfamiliar word from the dictionary or your reading, and challenge yourself to use it in your writing.

who struggled during their freshman year didn't put much thought into time management. Students who did manage their time had a smoother transition from high school to college.

A paper or digital planner, which visually highlights key academic dates, is a great time management tool for college. A planner keeps all of your academic dates in one handy location. Along with the planner, reading the syllabus for each of your courses will help you stay on track. The syllabus summarizes important information about the course, including the overall goals of the course and the topics that will be covered each week. The syllabus lists the dates of tests and quizzes and tells you when reading and homework assignments are due. Write down or enter these dates, along with the name of the course, in your planner.

Once you have key dates noted, it's important to prioritize your tasks. Ask yourself what needs to be done first, what should be done next, and so on. Breaking down your assignments into smaller parts can help you feel less overwhelmed. Always overestimate the amount of time you'll need for each task. Doing so will give you extra time to perfect your task or give you a cushion in case things don't go as planned.

When beginning your work, consider starting with the most difficult tasks; the rest of your to-do list won't be as daunting. Alternatively, getting some easy tasks out of the way first can give you a sense of accomplishment and keep you motivated. Find what works best for you.

Now that you know what you need to do and have allotted the time to do it, stay focused. It's easy to be distracted by friends, a favorite television show, e-mails, or phone calls. Before you know it, the time set aside to study or work on an assignment is gone, and you can't get that time back.

One way to keep track of upcoming tests and assignments is to use a paper planner. Jotting down academic deadlines and other commitments will help you manage your time effectively.

Note-Taking Tips

There are various note-taking systems out there. For example, the sentence method involves writing down every new fact, thought, or topic on its own line. With the outlining method, major points are written to the far left and more specific points are indented to the right. Some students use different colored pens or highlighters to indicate the major points discussed. Find what works best for you by testing these options, researching others, or creating your own.

Regardless of which note-taking system you use, be sure your notes include key points, examples, arguments, and facts. If you don't take enough notes, you'll end up with more questions than answers when it is time to study. Alternatively, trying to capture every word is impossible, and it distracts you from the main ideas. Always pay attention, even if the speaker or the topic isn't exactly fascinating. If you tune out, your notes will suffer. Once you've finished taking notes, rewrite or edit them later that day when the lecture or discussion is still fresh in your mind. Not only does this give you the chance to better organize your notes, it also helps you retain the information.

Studying Tips

Developing and using good study habits goes a long way in achieving academic success. Finding a place to study that allows you to concentrate is essential. Try the school library or find a quiet spot in your residence hall. You also need to figure out a study system that works best for each subject. Flash cards might work well for one class whereas outlining might be ideal for another.

Consider joining or forming a study group. Being part of a study group lets you discuss homework with your peers,

There are various methods that students use to take notes. Find what works best for you. After your classes, review and organize your notes and make sure your writing is legible.

compare notes, ask questions, and learn from each other. According to Richard Light, students who gathered in study groups and talked about their homework were "far more engaged and far better prepared, and they learned significantly more."

Study groups are an effective way to learn course material. Members do their homework independently before meeting to discuss the work as a group.

Attending any review sessions your professor offers is also a good idea.

Once you've figured out where and how to study, make the time to do it. Use your planner to set aside blocks of time for

studying and stick to it. Avoid studying when you are too tired and definitely don't leave it all for the night before a test.

Writing Tips

While the thought of writing a college paper might seem overwhelming, it's easy to tackle once you divide the process into smaller steps. First, if it hasn't been assigned, decide on a topic. For inspiration, think about your interests and passions. Or scan the news for a topic that speaks to you and also relates to the course material.

Once you've settled on a topic, start gathering information. Your college library is a good place to start. Many college libraries offer training sessions

Preventing Plagiarism

Plagiarism occurs when you use other people's ideas or words without giving them the credit. You lead your audience to believe you came up with the information. One example of plagiarism is cutting and pasting material found on the Internet into your paper and not attributing the Web site. Another example is taking information in a book and using it word-for-word in your paper while passing it off as your own.

Regardless of the method, plagiarism is wrong. You not only risk failing your class or being expelled if you are caught, but you also cheat yourself out of an education. After all, the whole point of attending college is to learn and grow intellectually.

To avoid plagiarism, always let readers know the source of your information. Ways to do this include using footnotes, quotation marks, and citations. A footnote appears at the bottom of a page and cites a reference for something mentioned in the text above. Quotation marks are used when the exact words from a source appear within your paper. A works cited page lists sources used in researching your paper. Be sure to ask your professor which citation style you should use. You may need to refer to a style manual in order to format your references correctly. Giving readers the sources of your information takes time, so be sure to take this into account when doing your assignments.

to help you learn how to access their resources. For example, the librarians may explain how to find articles in academic journals. If you plan to do online research, be sure to use credible Web sites such as those of well-established organizations or governmental agencies. Avoid blogs or sites where anyone and everyone can post information, such as Wikipedia.

During the research process, be sure to take detailed notes. Creating an outline can be very helpful. An outline not only keeps notes organized, it will help you stay on track when it is time to write your paper. Once you are done researching your topic and gathering information, write a rough draft. Refer to your outline to make sure all your thoughts are included and are in the right order. Your paper should be an in-depth explanation of the information in your outline. Finally, read your rough draft and make any edits. Take breaks while editing and rewriting. Some time away can help you see mistakes you didn't catch the first time.

For Those with Learning Disabilities or Difficulties

College is a difficult transition for all students, but it poses additional challenges for those with learning disabilities or difficulties. If you fall into this category, taking a summer precollege program is a good idea. These programs allow you to take some short courses and give you an idea of what to expect as a college student. Some precollege programs are specifically designed for students with learning disabilities; some of these are limited to students who will be attending that institution. To find out if a precollege program is available at your school, contact the college's disability support services office.

You should also figure out successful ways to deal with the limitations of your learning skills. For example, if you struggle with writing, consider recording lectures or using a laptop. If taking exams is a problem area, you may need to ask for extra time or a separate room. For difficulties with reading comprehension, try using audio versions of texts. If you have trouble studying, you might need to work on improving time management and organizational skills.

Once you are enrolled, many colleges offer academic support services to all students. Be sure to familiarize yourself with the services available at the colleges you are considering. Support programs may include tutoring, writing centers, time management classes, or study skills workshops. Through its disability support services office, your college may also provide additional services specifically aimed at students with learning disabilities.

Designing Your Program

Part of the college experience includes designing an academic program that balances your interests and passions with your school's requirements. Introductory classes in subjects that your school requires, like math, English, and philosophy, are known as core curriculum courses. Typically, students are required to take some of these classes during their freshman year. Students also have the option of picking classes that interest them. These courses are known as electives. Before you decide on any classes, be sure to find out your school's core requirements and what electives you can take.

Creating Your Schedule

When determining your academic schedule, aim for a mix of classes. Your semester should be a blend of easy and challenging courses. You also want to strike a balance among reading- and writing-intensive classes and classes with more problem solving, such as mathematics. If it's available during your first semester, sign up for a class that covers the fundamentals of writing. You'll be doing a lot of writing in college, so taking a course like this will give you the foundation you need for your entire college experience.

When creating your schedule, try to reserve some blocks of free time throughout your week for coursework and extracurricular activities. Also, be honest with yourself. If you know you're not a morning person,

When choosing college courses, aim for a mix of challenging and easy classes. Also, make sure your class schedule allows for enough free time to study and work on assignments.

don't sign up for early classes. You'll only end up struggling to get to these classes on time or you won't be at your sharpest.

While it's admirable to try to take on as many credits as possible, this isn't necessarily the best strategy. College life is an adjustment—give yourself time to get used to it. Plus, a heavy course load typically leaves students feeling burned-out or exhausted. It also doesn't leave enough time to explore extracurricular options. More than likely, you'll also have trouble finding the time to get all of your homework done.

Once you've made a list of the classes you'd like to take, review your choices with your academic advisor. Keep in mind that when you are ready to register, some of your classes might not be available. Play it safe and have alternative choices selected.

Think you picked the wrong class? Don't panic. Colleges typically allow students a certain period of time to make changes to their class schedules. This period for dropping and adding classes usually occurs at the start of a semester. You should aim to add or drop courses during this time frame to avoid any penalties. If you miss the cutoff date, your next option, typically, is to withdraw from a class. A withdrawal isn't an ideal choice since it might stay on your permanent record. Before dropping any class, make sure doing so won't affect your status as a full-time student or your eligibility for financial aid.

Considering a Major

A major is a specific group of classes a student must take in order to graduate. Major classes focus on one main area of interest; when you graduate, you'll have a strong background in this area. While you don't need to choose your major right away, it's a good idea to start giving it some thought. You can start by researching the kinds of careers or jobs you can pursue with the

Types of College Classes

Below are some of the common types of courses you'll find at college:

Lectures. In lecture courses, the professor speaks to a large group of students. There is generally little interaction with the professor or with other students. Some lecture courses have a weekly "recitation" session, which is a discussion class with a smaller group of students led by a graduate teaching assistant.

Seminars. Typically, seminars are discussion-based courses. In seminars, small and less formal groups of students share ideas and information with their instructors.

Lab courses. Usually found within the science curriculum, lab courses entail hands-on, investigative research.

Performance. Typically students taking classes in music, dance, or theater arts deliver performances to showcase their skills and knowledge. Students sometimes critique one another's work.

Studio. These classes generally involve art and design and take place in a studio setting. Students taking studio classes typically work on individual projects.

Work/Study. Work/study programs involve off-campus fieldwork that complements classroom lectures.

majors you are considering. Ask yourself if any of the options appeal to you. Find upperclassmen who have declared each of the majors you are interested in, and ask them what they like and dislike about their majors. Reading the course descriptions in your college's catalog can also help narrow down your choices. Circle any courses that sound appealing and cross out the ones that don't. When you are done, go back through the catalog and look at your results. You might discover that the majority of classes you were drawn to belong to a specific major.

Switching Majors

If you're struggling in the classes you are taking for your major or discover you're absolutely uninspired, it might mean you need to switch majors. You wouldn't be the first student in the history of college to do this. Students who change their major at least once are more common than students who do not.

Before switching, make sure you understand what academic requirements you'll have to complete once you make the change. Also, find out if switching majors will affect your financial aid or the cost of your college experience. It's best to talk with your current major advisor or dean to find out if there are any policies or rules that prevent you from switching immediately. It's also a good idea to speak with an advisor in the new major to find out what needs to be done to make the switch successfully.

Doubling Up

At many colleges, students can sign up for dual or double majors. A dual major lets you study two majors that are related to one another. In this option, classes tend to overlap so you're not necessarily extending your college stay. A double major involves studying two separate majors and sometimes even earning two degrees. In this case, there might not be any overlap in classes, which means you'll have a more demanding schedule. If you don't declare a double major early on, it might take longer to graduate than the traditional four years.

Both options are worth considering if you are willing and able to take on the extra workload. Potential benefits include an enhanced academic experience and an edge when applying for jobs. On the downside, your heavy workload may mean less time for nonacademic activities or for taking electives that interest you. For these reasons, it's not a good idea to double up simply because you can't decide between two areas of interest.

Minors

A minor involves taking several classes—about half the amount you would take for a major—that focus on a specific subject area. You can choose a minor that complements the major you have declared. For example, if you are majoring in communications, a minor in journalism can enhance your writing skills. Or, you can use a minor to explore a completely different passion. For instance, a student majoring in environmental studies can use a minor to satisfy an interest in music. Whether your minor complements your major or not, choosing one can give you an edge when it is time to search for a job. A minor can also add to your academic experience by exposing you to an area of knowledge beyond your major and broadening your interaction with students and staff.

Ten Great Questions
TO ASK UPPERCLASSMEN ABOUT COLLEGE LIFE

1 What academic advice do you have for my first semester?

2 How can I make new friends?

3 Is it normal to feel homesick?

4 What do you like/dislike about this college?

5 What was the biggest misconception you had about college?

6 How do you handle stress?

7 How do you handle peer pressure?

8 Where can I get help for personal problems or academic issues?

9 How do you successfully juggle your academic and social life?

10 What are some ways to stay safe on campus?

Chapter 3

Beyond the Classroom

The college experience is all about learning—and not just in the classroom. Getting involved in extra-curricular activities allows you to apply in-class learning to situations outside of the classroom. You also get the benefits of interacting with new people, developing new skills, doing something fun, and learning more about yourself and others. In fact, not getting involved could leave you feeling unsatisfied with your college experience. Professor Richard Light writes, "Students involved in some outside-of-classroom activities are far happier with their college experience than the few who are not involved." Below are some ways to make your college experience a richer and happier one.

Clubs and Organizations

Unlike in high school, clubs and organizations in college are run entirely by students. On-campus clubs and organizations are a great way to pursue an interest, whether it's something you are studying or not. Have a love of music? Look into joining the college radio station or singing in an a cappella group. Want to test out the field of politics? Become active in the student government. By getting involved in a club or organization, you'll satisfy an existing interest or possibly discover a new passion. Joining a club or organization also helps when it comes to meeting

College students perform a scene from a production of *The Foreigner*. Extracurricular activities can develop or uncover new skills.

new people and developing relationships. Club participation can also serve as a career boost. For example, a drama major who performs in college productions will have the advantage of experience in the field, when compared to a student who only takes courses.

Community Service

Community service is another way to get involved in a satisfying activity outside of the classroom. Community work allows you to help others and learn more about important public issues. Working with groups of people in communities beyond your

Community service allows you to help others while getting involved beyond the classroom. Above, college students help repair homes destroyed by Hurricane Katrina in New Orleans.

campus also fosters a better understanding of others. You can even test out career options through community service. For example, if you have an interest in medicine, you can volunteer your time at a local hospital. Another benefit of community service is the chance to interact with professionals in the field, people who could potentially serve as mentors.

Internships

An internship involves working for an employer (usually for free) in a career field that interests you. It allows you to apply your

As an intern, you can test out a career, apply your knowledge, and establish professional contacts. An internship might confirm your career path or lead you to a new one.

classroom learning in a real-world, professional environment. As an intern, you gain hands-on knowledge and develop new skills. Internships let you learn about a career by living it. When you work as an intern for an organization, you get to see what the working environment and daily tasks in a field are really like. You'll also polish your communication skills and learn how to present yourself in an adult, professional manner.

Internships are also an excellent way to make contacts within an industry. Such networking opportunities might lead to job prospects once you finish college. Companies sometimes use internships as a way to test out a potential employee for a position they expect to fill. Or you might make such an impression that your employer will create a new position with you in mind.

Study Abroad

The term "study abroad" covers a variety of overseas educational opportunities, including international internships and classroom-based learning. In today's global environment, many employers value and look for international experience in potential employees. But studying abroad does more than look impressive on your résumé. Studying abroad exposes you to different ways of life, making you more culturally aware. Further, you have the opportunity to learn about international problems and issues firsthand.

Studying abroad also offers the chance for personal growth. Managing travel and daily living far away from your routine life can

Tips on Selecting a Club

- Ask yourself what your interests are and what you enjoy doing. Search for a club that supports your answers.
- Review the list of clubs offered at your college. Look into the ones that sound appealing.
- Attend a meeting or ask peers already in clubs for their feedback.
- If you don't find a club that appeals to you, consider starting your own! There may be other students with the same interest, and you will develop your leadership skills.

boost your self-confidence and your sense of independence. The experience can even give you a new outlook on your own background. You might discover the reasons behind your family's cultural traditions from those living in the country of your ancestors. Or you might discover you have more in common with other cultures than you initially thought.

Sports

Being a part of a collegiate team is another way to get involved outside of the classroom. As a collegiate athlete, you'll spend time

One way to get involved outside of the classroom is by playing a sport, such as football. Joining a team requires a time commitment and can lead to lasting friendships.

practicing, traveling, and competing. It's also a great way to meet new people. Given how much time you spend with your teammates, it's likely you will establish some solid friendships among them.

Didn't make the varsity team? You can still get involved in sports while attending college. Club teams allow you to compete against other colleges without the major commitment required of a varsity team. In intramural sports, students from the same school compete against one another in different leagues. Pickup games are ideal if you don't want to make a team commitment but are looking for some sports action. You can typically find a game by checking campus fields and gym facilities, local parks, or bulletin boards. By taking part in sports, you'll not only get some exercise and meet new people, you'll also burn off stress—something you'll experience often as a college student.

Fraternities and Sororities

Another extracurricular option is joining a fraternity or sorority, which are clublike organizations that use Greek letters as their names. Fraternities are for men, and sororities are for women. As a member, you have the chance to meet new people and develop friendships that can last a lifetime. You can also gain leadership experience by helping oversee the various events that these organizations arrange. On the downside, going Greek can mean a hefty time commitment. Functions, meetings, community service requirements, and social activities all add up. Being a member of a Greek organization also costs money, including initiation fees and dues.

Joining a fraternity or sorority involves an invitation-only process that begins with rushing. Students use the rush

Joining a Greek organization can help you gain leadership experience and meet new people. Below, students gather outside a University of California, Berkeley, fraternity house.

period to learn more about the organization they are considering, including its history, members, and traditions. The pledge period begins when a student accepts an invitation, or bid, to join the group. A student is initiated into the organization at the end of the pledge period.

Unfortunately, some students seeking spots in fraternities and sororities make poor choices just to gain group approval. While it is not as common as it once was, hazing still takes place in some Greek organizations, particularly during the pledge period. According to the organization StopHazing.org, the term "hazing" refers to "any activity expected of someone joining a group (or to

Juggling It All

Do you think that taking on an extracurricular activity will have a negative impact on your grades? Think again. According to professor Richard Light's Harvard study, involvement in one or two activities "has little or no relationship to grades." This doesn't mean it's easy to juggle activities with academics. The following tips can help.

Plan ahead. If you know you have a major test in several weeks, plan to scale back your extracurricular commitments during this time. Instead of saying yes to chairing a club committee or organizing a pickup game, let someone else have a turn.

Stay focused. If extracurricular activities are taking time needed for your academics, it might be a sign you are overcommitted. Consider paring down your involvement with a group or dropping an activity completely.

Prioritize. If you're tapped to write a front-page story for the campus newspaper, go for it—as long as it won't interfere with other extracurricular obligations or your academics. Don't commit unless you know you can deliver without letting other areas suffer.

maintain full status in a group) that humiliates, degrades, or risks emotional and/or physical harm, regardless of the person's willingness to participate." Examples of hazing include verbal abuse, physical beatings, and binge drinking. Hazing incidents have even led to death.

If you find yourself in a situation where hazing is involved, leave and report it immediately. Of course, this may not be an easy choice. Some students fear retaliation if they speak up against the group. But not doing so could endanger your health or life, or the lives of others. It's better to take a stand—and leave to find people who treat you with respect—than to put up with hazing. If you become the victim of a hazing incident, seek counseling from on-campus or off-campus resources after you've reported the incident.

MYTHS and FACTS

MYTH If I mess up my freshman year, get a low grade, or drop out of a club, it will impact the rest of my life.

Fact Obviously, you should aim for high grades and explore extracurricular activities, but it's not going to ruin your entire college experience or your future career if you don't get it right during your first semester or two. Your freshman year is about trying things out, making mistakes, and, most important, learning from them.

MYTH I'm not going to fit in.

Fact While it's nice to think we are all extraordinarily unique, chances are there are other people at college who think like you do, have similar interests, or hold the same values. You might not meet them on your first day of school, but give it time. Help the process along by keeping an open mind and reaching out to people you never thought you'd connect with. In doing so, you just might surprise yourself.

MYTH I shouldn't go to college until I know what I want to do with the rest of my life.

Fact The majority of freshmen are undecided about their majors. You can use your freshman year to do some detective work. Sign up for classes that sound interesting, and explore various activities on campus. In doing so, you'll find out more about who you are and who you want to become.

Diversity and Living Arrangements

During your college years, you may have the chance to live away from home on a college campus. While the living options discussed below each have their pros and cons, most of them have a common benefit—the opportunity to interact with and learn about others.

Today, students from various racial, religious, ethnic, economic, and geographical backgrounds attend college. Consider this fact from the National Center for Education Statistics: Between 1976 and 2004, the undergraduate enrollment of minorities rose from 17 to 32 percent. The number of minority students attending college climbed from an estimated 1.5 million in 1976 to nearly 4.7 million in 2004.

Engaging and interacting with students from diverse backgrounds opens you up to an incredible learning opportunity. And what better way to learn than by living with other students? By immersing yourself in a diverse population, you expose yourself to different views, tastes, and preferences on a daily basis. You might learn about an author, musician, or culinary dish you hadn't heard of before. You also have the opportunity to witness the customs and traditions of others and learn about others' life experiences, beliefs, and political

Interacting with students from different ethnic and racial backgrounds is a key part of a rich and rewarding college experience.

views. Such moments enhance your overall learning and college experience.

In his book *Making the Most of College*, Richard Light wrote, "When students interact with fellow students from different racial and ethnic backgrounds in day-to-day living, it makes a strong impression." The experience may inspire insights about yourself or a change in your behavior. For example, you might think twice about casually using a derogatory term for an ethnic group if you witness firsthand how it can offend someone. No matter which living arrangement you choose, approach each person you meet with an open mind. You'll not only learn more about others, you'll also learn a great deal about yourself.

Residence Halls

In addition to exposing you to people of various backgrounds, living in a dormitory increases your chances of making friends and finding camaraderie. Often colleges will house freshmen on the same floors, which makes connecting with someone who is going through a similar experience much easier. Also, some dorms extend your learning through special programs; for example, a dorm with an arts theme may house students who share that interest.

The downside of living on campus is a lack of privacy; rooms are typically small, making it hard to have time alone. Also,

Living in a dorm room allows you to meet other students and boosts your chances of forming friendships. Dorms can be small spaces, however, so establish room rules to avoid conflict.

residence halls can sometimes be noisy. Finally, sharing your living space with one or more roommates can be rewarding, but it can also be a challenge. There is the very real possibility that you and your roommate won't see eye-to-eye on all matters. For tips on getting along with a roommate, refer to the sidebar on page 40.

Off-Campus Living

Living off campus allows you to reside with people you have chosen, and it could prove cheaper than living in residence halls. It may give you a greater feeling of independence and privacy—you might even have your own room. One major downside to off-campus accommodation is that it reduces your daily interaction with the large, diverse population of students you find on campus. You might even feel left out of the day-to-day happenings of campus life. It's worth weighing the pros and cons before making a decision. Below are some off-campus options.

Renting

Renting an apartment or a house is one way to live off campus. Just be sure this option won't stretch your budget. You'll need to take into account the costs associated with renting, such as utilities, food, and, of course, the rent. You'll also have to consider how you are going to acquire furnishings; buying a bed might be manageable, but buying all the basics for a kitchen might not. If your plan involves living with roommates, make sure they are trustworthy. Will they pay the rent on time? Will they honor the length of the lease? To find out about places to rent, ask your campus housing office for some leads;

Getting the keys to your own apartment or house is an exciting moment. But renting comes with serious responsibilities, such as finding dependable roommates, budgeting for bills, and making timely payments.

check local newspapers, Internet sites, and bulletin boards; or try roommate-locating services.

Sorority and Fraternity Houses

Some sororities and fraternities have houses on or near campus where members can live. This option might be cheaper than living on campus. It also provides you with a built-in support network of friends. The house might even be a charming historical structure. However, living in a sorority or fraternity house does have potential drawbacks. There's the possibility you'll be distracted by the social

Managing the Roommate Relationship

To reduce your chances of any dorm room conflicts, consider the following tips:

- Decide on rules regarding quiet hours, visitors or sleepovers, and borrowing. Honor these rules.
- Instead of immediately concluding that things aren't going to work out, try compromising first. For example, if you can't study when your roommate is on the phone, decide on a time when you both agree to be quiet and a time when your roommate can talk as loud as he or she wants.
- Let your roommate know sooner rather than later if there is a problem. If you communicate respectfully, your roommate will probably be responsive.
- If you feel you need help—or some moral support—when talking to your roommate about an issue, seek out your resident assistant (RA). He or she can sit in on the conversation or serve as a mediator.

Despite all the best efforts, in some cases you and your roommate might have to agree to disagree. Or the problems between you might be grounds for a room change. If, for example, your roommate is constantly interfering with your ability to study, look into the possibility of moving.

gatherings that commonly take place at such organizations or by the constant presence of friends. Also, living with a large group of students isn't typically associated with cleanliness. If you are a neat freak, this may not be a good option for you. Finally, once you factor in the cost of Greek membership, this might not be a financially attractive option after all.

Living at Home

Living at home while commuting to college definitely has its perks. One major benefit is the amount of money you will save in room and board fees. There's also something to be said for the comfort of home-cooked meals and familiar surroundings.

However, there are some downsides. For starters, you lose the opportunity to step outside of your comfort zone, personally and socially. Also, there may be the potential for conflict between you and your family. While you're striving to gain more independence, family members might keep treating you like a high school student. To prevent this problem, be sure you and your family share expectations and establish rules that suit everyone before you start college.

Finally, living at home might leave you feeling disconnected from campus life and your peers living on campus. Instead of going to class and coming straight home, make an extra effort to get involved with extracurricular activities. Also, find out if your school has any programs, clubs, or activities specifically geared toward commuters. If there aren't any, consider starting your own.

Chapter 5

Staying Healthy: Body and Mind

With so much to focus on at college—academics, extracurricular activities, and new friendships—it's easy to let your overall well-being take a backseat. But staying healthy, both physically and mentally, is just as important as finishing that term paper on time. By eating well, exercising regularly, and getting enough sleep, you'll be better equipped to handle the pressures and stresses of college life. You'll probably also prefer the way you look and feel.

It's common to feel stressed or anxious from time to time by the challenge of your first year of college. Taking on more responsibilities, juggling harder courses, and trying to fit in can make anyone feel overwhelmed. It becomes a problem when your feelings consume and take control of your life. If the college experience starts taking a toll on your physical or mental health, seek help immediately. Resources include your school's health services center and counseling services. By ignoring your health, you not only risk endangering yourself, but your academic success as well.

Nutrition

Eating right helps you maintain your weight, boosts your concentration, and keeps you healthy. It's also

College dining halls typically offer a variety of food choices in a buffet-style setting. Above, students at Dartmouth University have lunch at the campus cafeteria.

a great way to avoid the "freshman fifteen"—the dreaded weight gain students can experience during their first year at college. Don't think it can happen to you? The temptation to make poor food choices can be strong at college. School dining halls typically work like buffets, letting you eat whatever you want and as much as you want. Late-night pizza sessions and vending machine or food cart "meals" tend to be a college rite of passage. Throw in a decrease in physical activity (there is usually no required gym class and a lot more sitting around) and the pounds, well, add up. Fortunately, there's hope. As with other aspects of college life, when it comes to eating right, the decisions are yours to make. By following the tips below, you can stay healthy, feel energized, and avoid the freshman fifteen:

- Keep healthy snacks on hand if you plan to have a late-night study session. Fresh fruits and veggies or low-fat crackers are good options.
- Choose healthier versions of your favorite foods. For example, instead of whole-milk versions of cheese, try low-fat or nonfat alternatives.
- Limit how much you're eating. While it's tempting to sample the entire dining hall menu in one sitting, it's not healthy. Stick with serving-size portions instead.
- Don't skip meals. Missing meals will only make you eat more later.
- Watch what you drink. Sodas are high in sugar, and alcoholic drinks carry calories. Instead, grab a glass of water.
- Avoid eating large meals right before bedtime. Doing so can give you a restless night's sleep and can help pack on the pounds.

Eating Disorders

An eating disorder is a serious problem. If left untreated, it can cause death. On college campuses, eating disorders are more common among women than men. There are three types of eating disorders: anorexia nervosa involves the self-imposed restriction of food; bulimia nervosa involves excessive eating followed by an immediate purging of food; and binge-eating disorder involves compulsive overeating without purging.

Eating disorders often develop as a way to handle the pressures of life or to feel in control. If you think you or someone you know may have an eating disorder, get help. Reach out to your college's health services center, a resident assistant, or a trusted faculty member or friend.

Exercise

Not only will exercise help keep the freshman fifteen from your waistline, it will also go a long way in reducing stress, something every college student knows all too well. Exercise helps you stay in shape, and it's the perfect remedy when you need a study break.

There are several ways you can get some physical activity on campus. One option is to take a class that gets your heart rate moving. From volleyball to karate to yoga, colleges typically offer a variety of choices. You also can utilize your school's facilities. Most colleges have a weight room, a track, a fitness center, or an indoor swimming pool. Take advantage of these options. After all, your

Walking to classes and riding your bike around campus are two ways to fit exercise into your day.

tuition helps pay for these facilities! You also can run, walk, or cycle your way around campus. Taking part in a pickup game or joining an intramural team or club team are other ways to fit in exercise. Some gyms or fitness centers near campus may even offer student discounts.

It's up to you to make the time for exercise at college. Fortunately, staying fit doesn't have to consume a lot of time. Even something as simple as taking the stairs instead of the elevator makes a difference.

Mental Health Issues

Some mental health issues—like depression and anxiety—are common among college students. According to the book *Real College: The Essential Guide to Student Life*, depression affects

If you think you or someone you know is suffering from a mental health issue, seek out help immediately. One option is your college's health services center.

one in ten college students. People suffering from depression may feel overwhelmed, disconnected from the world, or despairing. In some cases, depression may even lead to thoughts of suicide. It's crucial to take such thoughts seriously: suicide is a leading cause of death among college students.

While some anxiety is normal, it becomes a problem when it keeps you from functioning. You may become so overwhelmed by anxiety that you have great difficulty sleeping, following a daily routine, studying, or interacting with others. Anxiety disorders are the most common mental illness in the nation.

Getting help for any mental health issue is crucial. You can start by speaking with an advisor or reading your college's printed or online materials to learn about your options. You also can turn to your school's health services center or counseling services for

Signs and Symptoms of Mental Health Problems

Below are some of the signs and symptoms of mental health disorders:

- Feelings of anger, rage, hopelessness, worthlessness, or constant exhaustion
- Changes in sleeping or eating patterns
- Withdrawal from people or activities
- Difficulty making decisions, concentrating, or remembering
- Changes—sometimes unsafe ones—in behavior (i.e., not bathing, irresponsible drinking)

If you recognize these symptoms in yourself, it's important to seek help. If you notice these symptoms in someone you know, encourage him or her to talk with a professional on campus about what he or she is feeling.

guidance. Most colleges have staff who are trained and experienced in helping students with these problems. Alternatively, you can reach out to a trusted faculty member who can either help or point you in the right direction.

Sleep

If you think skimping on sleep is a good way to make time for all of your college obligations, think again. If you don't get enough

Not getting enough sleep can result in trouble concentrating. Instead of pulling all-nighters and paying the price the next day, give yourself enough time to study and get a good night's rest.

shut-eye, you're more likely to make mistakes and have trouble concentrating—two things you don't want to happen when you are trying to ace a course. Lack of sleep also increases your risk of depression and weakens the immune system. When you're tired, you tend to make poor food choices and do less physical activity. You may also damage your relationships with others—no one likes a sleep-deprived, cranky roommate. Practice good sleeping habits while you are at college. Stick to a regular sleeping schedule and stay away from large meals or caffeine right before you go to bed.

Chapter 6

Making Good Choices About Sex, Drugs, and Drinking

Students attending college typically have more freedom in their personal lives than high school students. While exploring this independence is an important part of college life, so is making good choices. The pressure to fit in and impress your peers can make the decision-making process more complex. When in doubt, remain true to yourself and your values. If some of your peers aren't respecting your choices, find ones who do.

Sex

Regardless of what your friends may decide, choosing to have sex, abstain, or wait a while is a decision you have to make for yourself. Whatever your choice, be sure it's one you are comfortable with and not one you've been pressured into making. You also want to plan ahead in order to follow through on your decision. Going into situations emotionally prepared—and armed with knowledge—will help you stand by your decisions instead of second-guessing yourself.

If you decide to have sex, be sure to take responsibility for your health. Irresponsible sex—such as

If you choose to get involved with someone, clearly communicate your boundaries when it comes to sex. If you decide to become sexually active, be sure to do so responsibly.

unprotected sex—can result in serious consequences like unwanted pregnancies and sexually transmitted diseases (STDs). According to the Centers for Disease Control and Prevention (CDC), nearly half of the estimated nineteen million new cases of STDs reported each year infect people between the ages of fifteen and twenty-four. For this reason, college health services and other campus organizations often provide information and education to students about safe sex. If you are considering being sexually active at college, it is important to take advantage of these resources and educate yourself.

"Hooking Up"

Today, traditional dating on college campuses has been largely replaced with "hooking up." Rather than going on formal one-on-one dates, students attend parties and group outings; students who are attracted to one another may then have casual encounters. The meaning of the term "hooking up" depends on the student you're asking. It can mean anything from just kissing to having sex. The person you hook up with can be someone you just met or a familiar face. While some hookups lead to steady relationships, most of them don't. Since hooking up means something different to each person, there's the potential for misunderstandings and hurt feelings. If you do plan to hook up with someone, it's important to talk about your expectations beforehand.

Sexual Harassment and Date Rape

Unfortunately, sexual harassment can and does occur on college campuses. While sexual harassment can happen to women or men, women are typically the victims. Sexual harassment ranges from inappropriate comments to sexual assault.

Date rape is another real and potential threat to college students. Such attacks often occur between students who know each other. The victim is forced to have sex against his or her will after passing out from too much alcohol or when requests not to go further are ignored.

One of the best ways to avoid date rape is to discuss personal boundaries with a romantic interest before getting sexually involved. It's also important not to lose the ability to make decisions by having too much alcohol or by taking drugs. If, despite

The RAINN organization offers live and anonymous support through an online sexual assault hotline that works in a similar way to instant messaging. The free, secure hotline is available twenty-four hours a day.

setting ground rules with a person, you find your wishes are not being respected, leave. If you become the victim of a sexual attack, get help immediately. Seek out medical attention if you need it and contact campus police. Also, look into any support

Date Rape Drugs

Date rape drugs, such as Rohypnol (also known as "roofies") and gamma hydroxy butyrate, or GHB, are used to sedate victims before they are sexually assaulted. The drugs—which can be odorless and colorless—are typically slipped into the drinks of unknowing victims.

Stay safe by always keeping an eye on your drink. If someone you don't know offers you a drink—especially one that has already been poured or mixed—politely decline. Also, use the "buddy system" at parties and night spots. With trusted friends, plan to keep an eye on each other and walk home together.

services your college may offer and reach out to family and friends for their support.

Drugs

Drug use is another issue you could potentially face at college. Although the drugs of choice may vary from college to college, the consequences of taking them do not. The threat of getting injured, hurting others, or even dying is unfortunately very real.

Marijuana is one of the more prevalent drugs on college campuses. In a 2005 study conducted by the nonprofit Core Institute at Southern Illinois University, about 30 percent of college students admitted to using pot in the past year. The effects of using marijuana include decreases in attention and concentration and difficulty storing new information. These are definitely not effects you want when you are trying to learn!

Another common drug on the college scene is MDMA, or ecstasy. Both a stimulant and a psychedelic, ecstasy gives users a sense of alertness and energy. However, it can also cause jitteriness and teeth clenching and can lead to long-term effects on the brain. As with other drugs, an overdose can result in death. Some college students use methamphetamine, also known as crystal meth. This drug is a stimulant that can trigger aggressive and violent behavior in users.

Prescription drug abuse also happens on some campuses. With more and more people taking prescription medications for mood and attention disorders, such drugs are readily available and often shared among friends. Self-medicating for mood problems is never a good idea. Just because a drug works for the person for whom it was prescribed doesn't mean your body will react the same way. If you are having trouble with anxiety, sleep deprivation, or other issues, seek the help of a health care professional.

Drinking

Alcohol is the drug of choice on many college campuses. A depressant that sedates the central nervous system, alcohol affects your emotions, thoughts, and judgments. Alcohol can also cause you to have trouble speaking, standing, walking, or driving. As a result, drunken students are more likely to hurt themselves or others. In incidents of sexual assault, rape, assault, and trouble with the law, college students under the

Dangers of Drinking for Women

While the dangers of alcohol apply to both men and women, alcohol poses additional risks for women:

- Women tend to be smaller than men and produce less of the enzyme that metabolizes alcohol; therefore, they tend to feel the effects of alcohol more quickly.
- The risk of sexual abuse and assault increases the more a woman drinks.
- Women who drink heavily are more likely to have unprotected sex.

influence are often involved. Too much alcohol can even result in death.

Alcohol can have a negative impact on learning. According to Henry Wechsler and Bernice Wuethrich in their book *Dying to Drink*, "Because the human brain continues to develop into a person's twenties, excessive drinking even in college has the potential to destroy a significant amount of mental capacity." The dangers of alcohol increase for students who are binge drinkers. The National Institute of Alcohol and Alcoholism describes binge drinking as consuming five or more successive drinks for men and four or more drinks for women. Compared to students who drink moderately, binge drinkers are more likely to drive drunk, hurt themselves, have unprotected sex, damage property, get into arguments, and fall behind in schoolwork.

Navigating these issues can be tough; trying to make a good decision with the added pressure of fitting in is even tougher. To make well-informed choices, arm yourself with knowledge and stand behind your values and beliefs. Remember, your decisions and actions involving sex, drugs, and alcohol carry serious consequences. Make good choices.

Chapter 7

Making and Managing Money

From tuition to room and board to books, college costs add up quickly. You'll probably be responsible for helping to cover some of these costs. One way to do this is to work while going to school, either on or off campus.

On-Campus Work

To find out about work opportunities on campus, visit your school's student employment office. Options may include working for the art center, serving as a college tour guide, or manning the desk of a residence hall. The benefits of working on campus include a short commute and the potential to meet and interact with other students. Also, your employer will probably understand when you need to focus on academics. You might even enjoy job perks, such as free tickets at the arts center where you work. On the other hand, you may earn less than you would at an off-campus job. Also, studying, living, and working in the same environment might become monotonous.

Off-Campus Work

For a job off campus, check local newspaper and Internet ads or simply walk into an establishment

Landing a job on campus means more interaction with fellow students and a short commute. Plus, your employer will be more likely to understand if you need to take time off for academics.

and ask if they are hiring. The benefits of off-campus work include the potential to earn more money and meet people outside of the college community. The job might even include an employee discount on items you need or want. One drawback is that you'll need to organize, and pay for, transportation to and from an off-campus job. Also, off-campus employers might not be as understanding when you need to take time off to focus on school.

Federal Work-Study Program

The federal work-study program is another way to earn money while going to college. The program is geared toward students with financial need. In addition to performing needed services on campus, students in the program may do jobs that are related to their field of study or that help the community. The amount of aid you receive depends on your family's income, how much you get in other forms of financial assistance, and available school funds. The program is campus-based; the participating schools manage it. Not all colleges take part in this program, so be sure to check if your college does.

Alternative Sources of Income

For those hoping to make some money without taking on a steady commitment, creativity is key. Try selling items you no longer need or use. Post flyers or go online to sites like eBay and Craigslist. You could also earn money by participating in research studies conducted by college departments, such as psychology and behavioral studies. There may be money-earning potential in your academic talents, too. For instance,

Balancing Work and School

Whether you need to work or just want some spending money, it's important not to let your job get in the way of your academics. Here are some ways to balance the two commitments:

- Find an employer who is flexible and who understands that you need to put your academics first.
- Consider working more hours at the start of the year, when academic programs tend to be less demanding.
- Alternatively, consider starting out with a few hours and increasing your time commitment gradually to make sure you can handle it.
- Most on-campus jobs limit students to working a maximum of twenty hours a week. Apply the same limit to an off-campus job.
- Give yourself some time off. If you spend every available moment either working or studying, you are going to burn out. Leave yourself with a free day or night when you can relax and recharge.
- If your grades are slipping, consider reducing your work hours. Another option is to postpone working until the summer when you won't have to juggle a job with academics.

if you are a strong writer, consider editing papers or crafting résumés for a fee. If you like kids, area parents might need a tutor or babysitter for their school-age children.

Managing Money

Now that you are making money, you'll need to manage it. A budget is a great way to keep track of how much money is coming in and how much is going out.

To create a budget, start by listing all of the expenses you will be expected to handle during a semester. Remember to allow yourself a responsible amount for social activities and entertainment. When you are finished listing your expenses, figure out ways to lower them. For example, if you have a great cell phone plan, you might not need a land line in your room. Next, list your sources of income (i.e., financial aid, work, parents) and the amount of income you can expect from each. Compare your income for a semester with your expenses. If your expenses are more than your income, you'll have to trim costs further or figure out how to bring in more money. Your aim is to have more money coming in than going out.

Once you have a realistic budget, stick to it! To help with this, pay for items in cash whenever you can. It gives you a much better sense of how much spending money you really have. Keep track of how much you spend monthly in each of your expense categories. Monitor yourself to be sure you are not spending more than your budget allows. When you have reached your monthly limit for a category, such as eating out, you should stop spending money in that area. However, if you do spend more than you planned in one area, compensate by spending less than you planned in another.

Part of creating a budget involves adding up all of your expenses. To stay within your budget, be sure to keep tabs on your spending.

Avoiding Debt

College students typically get flooded with credit card offers. Before you say yes to that piece of plastic, weigh the pros and cons. A credit card can be convenient when you need to make a purchase but your financial aid hasn't arrived yet or you're waiting for your paycheck to clear. Credit cards can also come in handy in emergencies, such as a car breakdown. If used wisely, a credit card can help you establish a good credit history.

However, credit card balances can add up quickly. Before you know it, you could owe thousands and find yourself struggling just to make the minimum payments. A 2004 study by student loan lender Nellie Mae found that the average outstanding balance on college students' credit cards was $2,169. For 23 percent of students surveyed, balances were more than $3,000. More than 50 percent of students did not pay off their cards in full each month. Credit card companies penalize customers with finance charges and late fees for carrying a balance or missing a payment, so these cards can become even more expensive.

Taking out a student loan would be a wiser move because loans offer lower interest rates. Finance charges, late fees, and high interest rates make it harder to pay off a credit card. As a result, if you create a large debt by charging your tuition or by spending irresponsibly at college, you may carry this burden for years after you graduate.

If you want the convenience of a credit card but without the risk, there is another option: the debit card. A debit card works—and looks—just like a credit card. The major difference between a debit card and a credit card is that the money you "charge" on your debit card comes out of your checking account. This means you can only spend what you have in your bank account. In this way, it is similar to paying in cash. A debit card can offer you the ease of a credit card without the threat of debt.

When it comes to credit card debt, the best advice is not to have any. But if you find yourself in trouble, don't wait to get help. Reach out to your parents, speak with a financial counselor at your college, or explore nonprofit organizations that can help you get a handle on your debt.

Parting Words

While college offers a more demanding and challenging pace than high school, it also brings countless opportunities. From discovering your future career to shaping your identity, the possibilities are endless. As you start your first year of college, work hard, embrace opportunities for growth, and enjoy the rewards.

Glossary

anorexia nervosa A condition that involves strictly limiting food intake, extreme weight loss, and a distorted self-image. People with this condition might follow rigid rules regarding what and when to eat.

anxiety Feelings of uneasiness and worry.

anxiety disorder A condition in which a person experiences more anxiety than what is appropriate for a situation.

balance The amount of money you have in a bank account.

binge-eating disorder A condition that involves overeating without purging. Following a binge session, people with this condition tend to feel self-loathing, misery, and guilt.

budget A plan that keeps track of expenses and income.

bulimia nervosa A condition that involves overeating followed by purging. Purging methods include vomiting or the use of laxatives.

core curriculum Courses in basic subjects that students are required to take.

credit An arrangement in which a borrower receives goods or services using the money of a lender and agrees to pay back the lender at a later date.

credit card Issued by a bank or business, a card that is used to buy goods or services on credit.

depression A medical illness that negatively affects one's outlook and behavior. Someone with depression might experience fatigue, despair, dread, and hopelessness.

electives Courses that students are not required to take. Students sign up for these courses out of an interest or curiosity in the subject matter.

finance charge Any charge imposed for the use of credit.

interest rate A percentage that is charged or paid for the use of money.

major   A group of college courses that deal with a specific academic subject. A major allows a student to learn about a field of interest in-depth.

minor   Several classes that deal with a specific academic subject. A minor can go hand-in-hand with a major or it can be completely unrelated to it.

sexually transmitted disease (STD)   A disease that is typically caught through intimate sexual contact. Types of STDs include chlamydia, gonorrhea, and syphilis.

study group   A small group formed by students in the same class that meets regularly to discuss homework and study for exams. Before meeting as a group, each member does his or her own homework.

syllabus   A document that provides information about a course, such as key dates, grading policy, the professor's contact information and expectations of students, and a description of the course and its objectives. The information contained in a syllabus varies from course to course and professor to professor.

AmeriCorps
1201 New York Avenue NW
Washington, DC 20525
(202) 606-5000
Web site: http://www.americorps.org
AmeriCorps offers volunteer opportunities through a partnership
with local and national nonprofit groups. Opportunities
range from tutoring disadvantaged youth to teaching
computer skills.

Centre for Addiction and Mental Health (CAMH)
250 College Street
Toronto, ON M5T 1R8
Canada
(800) 463-6273
Web site: http://www.camh.net
Canada's leading mental health and addiction organization,
CAMH provides information on various mental health issues.

Council on International Educational Exchange (CIEE)
300 Fore Street
Portland, ME 04101
(800) 40-STUDY (407-8839)
Web site: http://www.ciee.org
A nongovernmental organization, CIEE creates and administers
programs that include study abroad opportunities for college
students.

George Washington University
HEATH Resource Center
2134 G Street NW

Washington, DC 20052-0001

Web site: http://www.heath.gwu.edu

The HEATH Resource Center is an online clearinghouse on postsecondary education for students with disabilities. The site offers information on various topics, such as classroom adaptations, transition resources, and career development.

Mental Health America

2000 N. Beauregard Street, 6th Floor

Alexandria, VA 22311

(800) 969-6642

Web site: http://www.mentalhealthamerica.net

Mental Health America is a nonprofit that offers information about mental health issues and conditions. The organization also provides various resources for those seeking help.

National Center for Learning Disabilities

381 Park Avenue South, Suite 1401

New York, NY 10016

(888) 575-7373

Web site: http://www.NCLD.org

The National Center for Learning Disabilities offers information about learning resources and learning disabilities, promotes research efforts, and advocates for those with learning disabilities. The site includes information about transitioning to college.

National Eating Disorders Association

603 Stewart Street, Suite 803

Seattle, WA 98101

(206) 382-3587

Information and referral helpline: (800) 931-2237
Web site: http://www.nationaleatingdisorders.org
The National Eating Disorders Association provides information, resources, and support to those who have eating disorders and to their families and friends.

National Foundation for Credit Counseling (NFCC)
801 Roeder Road, Suite 900
Silver Spring, MD 20910
(301) 589-5600
Web site: http://www.nfcc.org
A credit counseling organization, the NFCC—through its member agencies—offers services (at low or no cost) that include budget education and debt management plans. The Web site also includes advice on handling debt.

Rape, Abuse & Incest National Network (RAINN)
2000 L Street NW, Suite 406
Washington, DC 20036
(202) 544-3064
National sexual assault hotline: (800) 656-HOPE (4673)
Web site: http://www.rainn.org
A nonprofit organization, RAINN provides free, confidential counseling twenty-four hours a day, regardless of where you reside in the country. The group's Web site includes a section for college students who want to get involved or learn more.

Volunteer Canada
353 Dalhousie Street, 3rd Floor
Ottawa, ON K1N 7G1

Canada
(800) 670-0401
Web site: http://www.volunteer.ca
Volunteer Canada promotes volunteerism and civic participation
through programs, projects, initiatives, and training throughout Canada. The group's site links users to various volunteer
centers throughout the nation.

Web Sites

Due to the changing nature of Internet links, Rosen Publishing
has developed an online list of Web sites related to the subject
of this book. This site is updated regularly. Please use this link
to access this list:

http://www.rosenlinks.com/col/yfyc

For Further Reading

College Board. *Book of Majors 2009* (College Board Index of Majors and Graduate Degrees). New York, NY: College Board, 2008.

Kadar, Andrew G. *College Life 102: The No-Bull Guide to a Great Freshman Year*. Lincoln, NE: iUniverse, Inc., 2006.

Knox, Susan. *Financial Basics: A Money-Management Guide for Students*. Columbus, OH: Ohio State University Press, 2004.

Newport, Cal. *How to Become a Straight-A Student: The Unconventional Strategies Real College Students Use to Score High While Studying Less*. New York, NY: Broadway Books, 2007.

Nist-Olejnik, Sherrie, and Jodi Patrick Holschuh. *College Rules! How to Study, Survive, and Succeed in College*. 2nd ed. Berkeley, CA: Ten Speed Press, 2007.

Seghers, Linda, ed. *Colleges for Students with Learning Disabilities and ADD*. 8th ed. Lawrenceville, NJ: Peterson's, 2007.

Smith, M. J., and Fred Smith. *The Smart Student's Guide to Healthy Living: How to Survive Stress, Late Nights, and the College Cafeteria*. Oakland, CA: New Harbinger Publications, 2006.

Vye, Christopher, Kathlene Scholljegerdes, and I. David Welch. *Under Pressure and Overwhelmed: Coping with Anxiety in College*. New York, NY: Praeger Publishers, 2007.

Wider, Jennifer. *The Doctor's Complete College Girls' Health Guide: From Sex to Drugs to the Freshman 15*. New York, NY: Bantam Books, 2006.

Active Minds. "What to Look For." Retrieved February 23, 2009 (http://www.activeminds.org/index.php?option=com_content&task=view&id=49&Itemid=79>).

Bogle, Kathleen A. *Hooking Up: Sex, Dating, and Relationships on Campus*. New York, NY: New York University Press, 2008.

California Polytechnic State University. "Notetaking Systems." Retrieved February 23, 2009 (http://sas.calpoly.edu/asc/ssl/notetaking.systems.html).

Centers for Disease Control and Prevention. "Sexually Transmitted Disease Surveillance, 2007." December 2008. Retrieved February 28, 2009 (http://www.cdc.gov/std/stats07/toc.htm).

CollegeTips.com. "Eating Disorders and College Students." Retrieved February 23, 2009 (http://www.collegetips.com/college-health/eating-disorders.php).

Core Institute at Southern Illinois University. "The Core Alcohol and Drug Survey." 2005. Retrieved February 28, 2009 (http://www.siu.edu/departments/coreinst/public_html).

Couch, Christina. "Fight Back." CollegeView.com. Retrieved February 23, 2009 (http://www.collegeview.com/articles/CV/campuslife/fight_back.html).

Diehl, Chris. "Alternative Sources of Income for Students." FastWeb.com. Retrieved February 23, 2009 (http://www.fastweb.com/fastweb/resources/articles/index/110293?).

Diehl, Chris. "A Major Switch." FastWeb.com. Retrieved February 23, 2009 (http://www.fastweb.com/fastweb/resources/articles/index/110254?).

Drill, Esther, Heather McDonald, and Rebecca Odes. *Where Do I Go from Here? Getting a Life After High School*. New York, NY: Penguin Group (USA), 2004.

FastWeb.com. "Writing Panic: Making It Count." Retrieved February 23, 2009 (http://www.fastweb.com/fastweb/ resources/articles/index/110641).

Federal Student Aid. "Campus-Based Aid." Retrieved February 23, 2009 (http://studentaid.ed.gov/PORTALSWebApp/ students/english/campusaid.jsp).

Fives, Theresa, and Holly Popowski. *Getting Through College Without Going Broke*. New York, NY: Natavi Guides, 2003.

Hadad, Roxana. "Study Abroad Basics." FastWeb.com. Retrieved February 23, 2009 (http://www.fastweb.com/ fastweb/resources/articles/index/100521?).

Hansen, Katharine. "The Course Syllabus: Know It, Love It, Understand It, Benefit from It." MyCollegeSuccessStory. com. Retrieved February 23, 2009 (http://www. mycollegesuccessstory.com/academic-success-tools/ course-syllabus.html).

Hansen, Katharine. "10 Tips for Time Management." MyCollegeSuccessStory.com. Retrieved February 23, 2009 (http://www.mycollegesuccessstory.com/ academic-success-tools/time-management-tips.html).

Hansen, Randall S. "College Study Do's and Don'ts: Tips for Thriving in College." MyCollegeSuccessStory. com. Retrieved February 23, 2009 (http://www. mycollegesuccessstory.com/academic-success-tools/ college-studying-dos-donts.html).

Hansen, Randall S. "Effective Note-Taking: Critical Note-Taking Do's and Don'ts." MyCollegeSuccessStory.com. Retrieved February 23, 2009 (http://www.mycollegesuccessstory.com/ academic-success-tools/effective-note-taking.html).

Jed Foundation. "Learn More: About Our Cause." Retrieved February 23, 2009 (http://www.jedfoundation.org/learn-more/about-our-cause).

Jed Foundation. "Learn More: Anxiety." Retrieved February 23, 2009 (http://www.jedfoundation.org/learn-more/anxiety).

Jones, Jane S. "College Greek Life 101: A Primer About Fraternities and Sororities." CollegeView.com. Retrieved February 23, 2009 (http://www.collegeview.com/articles/CV/campuslife/fraternities_and_sororities.html).

KewalRamani, Angelina, Lauren Gilbertson, Mary Ann Fox, and Stephen Provasnik. "Status and Trends in the Education of Racial and Ethnic Minorities." National Center for Education Statistics, September 12, 2007. Retrieved February 23, 2009 (http://nces.ed.gov/pubSearch/pubsinfo.asp?pubid=2007039).

Kronish, Elisa. "Double Majors Do Double Duty." FastWeb.com. Retrieved February 23, 2009 (http://www.fastweb.com/fastweb/resources/articles/index/100841).

Kuhn, Cynthia, Scott Swartzwelder, and Wilkie Wilson. *Buzzed: The Straight Facts About the Most Used and Abused Drugs from Alcohol to Ecstasy*. 3rd Edition. New York, NY: W. W. Norton & Company, 2008.

Kulla, Bridget. "Five Health Mistakes College Students Make." FastWeb.com. Retrieved February 23, 2009 (http://www.fastweb.com/fastweb/resources/articles/index/110289).

Light, Richard J. *Making the Most of College: Students Speak Their Minds*. Cambridge, MA: Harvard University Press, 2001.

Lombardo, Allison. *Navigating Your Freshman Year*. New York, NY: Natavi Guides, 2003.

Murray, Lori. "Class Scheduling Do's and Don'ts for First-Year Students." CollegeView.com. Retrieved February 23, 2009 (http://www.collegeview.com/articles/CV/campuslife/scheduling-classes.html).

Muskingum College Center for Advancement of Learning. "Learning Strategies Database: Students." Retrieved February 23, 2009 (http://www.muskingum.edu/~cal/database/tocollege/index_students.html).

National Center for Learning Disabilities. "Transition to College: Strategic Planning to Ensure Success for Students with Learning Disabilities." Retrieved May 10, 2009 (http://www.ncld.org/images/stories/downloads/parent_center/transition_to_college.pdf).

Nellie Mae. "College Students Get Wise About Credit Cards." May 25, 2005. Retrieved February 23, 2009 (http://www.nelliemae.com/aboutus/collegestudentswise052505.html).

Nuwer, Hank. *The Hazing Reader*. Bloomington, IN: Indiana University Press, 2004.

Paulsen, Kenneth J. *Living the College Life: Real Students. Real Experiences. Real Advice*. Hoboken, NJ: Wiley Publishing, 2005.

Peterson, Kay. "Working for Free: The Benefits of Internships." FastWeb.com. Retrieved February 23, 2009 (http://www.fastweb.com/fastweb/resources/articles/index/100010?).

Pohl, Laura. "Give Me Some Credit." FastWeb.com. Retrieved February 23, 2009 (http://www.fastweb.com/fastweb/resources/articles/index/100003).

Pupillo, Jessica. "The Value of Volunteering." CollegeView.com. Retrieved February 23, 2009 (http://www.collegeview.com/articles/CV/campuslife/value_of_volunteering.html).

Raskin, Robin. *Parents' Guide to College Life: 181 Straight Answers on Everything You Can Expect Over the Next Four Years*. New York, NY: Princeton Review, 2006.

Stone, Douglas, and Elizabeth Tippett. *Real College: The Essential Guide to Student Life*. New York, NY: Penguin Group (USA), 2004.

StopHazing.org. "Hazing Defined." Retrieved February 23, 2009 (http://www.stophazing.org/definition.html).

Wechsler, Henry, and Bernice Wuethrich. *Dying to Drink: Confronting Binge Drinking on College Campuses*. New York, NY: Rodale, 2002.

Wheatt, Dalia. "Avoiding the Freshman 15." CollegeView.com. Retrieved February 23, 2009 (http://www.collegeview.com/articles/CV/campuslife/avoiding_freshman15.html).

Index

About the Author

Maria DaSilva-Gordon drew from her positive experiences attending a community college and a university for this book. As a college student, she received awards for outstanding academic achievement, aptitude in the field of writing, and excellence in the study of journalism. She graduated magna cum laude. Both of her college internships led to rewarding job opportunities. Through extracurricular activities, she formed friendships that continue to thrive today. A former newspaper reporter, she spends her time writing for newspapers, trade publications, and the occasional Web site. She also teaches journalism workshops to students of various learning abilities and grade levels through her business, Making Headlines, LLC.

Photo Credits

Cover, pp. 1, 59 © www.istockphoto.com/Chris Schmidt; p. 5 © www.istockphoto.com/Oleg Prikhodko; pp. 7, 14, 20, 28, 32, 40, 45, 48, 54, 56, 61 © www.istockphoto.com/Robert Dant; pp. 9, 11, 63 © www.istockphoto.com; pp. 12–13, 27, 36, 49, 51 Shutterstock; p.18 © Michael Newman/Photo Edit; p. 25 © Tony Freeman/Photo Edit; p. 26 © Marty Heitner/Image Works; p. 29 © www.istockphoto.com/James Booulette; pp. © 31, 43 David Young-Wolff/Photo Edit; p. 37 © Andy Sacks/Photo Edit; p. 39 © Cleve Bryant/Photo Edit; p. 46 © William Thomas/Getty Images; p. 47 © www.istockphoto.com/Joselito Briones.

Designer: Nicole Russo; Editor: Andrea Sclarow;
Photo Researcher: Marty Levick